HEALTHY DOG FOOD

COOKBOOK AND FOOD LIST

Enhance your furry friend's longevity and well-being with tasty and nutritious home-made recipes

Dr. VICTORIA H. MILLER

TABLE OF CONTENTS

INTRODUCTION 9

The Importance of a Balanced Diet for Dogs
....9

Understanding Your Dog's Nutritional Needs
....11

Benefits of Homemade Dog Food 15

Getting Started 19

Kitchen Essentials for Homemade Dog Food
....19

Safe and Unsafe Ingredients for Dogs 23

Safe Ingredients for Dogs 24

Unsafe Ingredients for Dogs 25

How to Transition Your Dog to Homemade
Meals 27

Nutrition Basics 32

The Role of Proteins, Carbohydrates, and
Fats 32

Proteins 32

Carbohydrates 34

Fats.. 35

Vitamins and Minerals: What Your Dog
Needs.................................... 36

Hydration: Ensuring Your Dog Gets Enough
Water 40

Chapter 4 45

**Simple Starters Easy Recipes for Beginners
.... 45**

Chicken and Rice Delight........................ 45

Beefy Veggie Mix.......................... 46

Turkey and Pea Pod Pottage 47

Salmon Sweet Potato Hash 47

Simple Chicken Broth Soup 48

Easy Egg and Potato Scramble 49

Puppy Pumpkin Rice 50

Veggie Beef Bliss.................................50

Fisherman's Feast 51

Canine Cottage Pie...........................52

Protein Power: Meat, Fish, and Egg Recipes

...53

Classic Beef Stew 53

Chicken & Quinoa Dinner 54

Salmon Rice Bowl..............................55

Turkey and Vegetable Loaf 55

Beefy Pumpkin Mash 56

Egg & Veggie Scramble...........................57

Sardine Delight 58

Liver and Lentil Stew 59

Chicken and Egg Breakfast Patties...........59

Tuna and Sweet Potato Balls 60

Vegetarian Options for Dogs 62

Sweet Potato and Lentil Loaf....................62

Quinoa Veggie Patties 63

Pumpkin Rice Pudding 64

Tofu and Vegetable Stir-fry 65

Peanut Butter Oatmeal Cookies 66

Veggie Doggie Chili 67

Cheesy Veggie Muffins 67

Spinach and Cottage Cheese Balls 68

Sweet Pea and Carrot Mash 69

Butternut Squash and Apple Puree 70

Grain-Free Meals for Sensitive Stomachs. 71

Chicken and Sweet Potato Stew 71

Beef and Pumpkin Dinner 72

Salmon and Zucchini Hash 73

Turkey and Carrot Patties 74

Lamb and Pea Puree 75

Egg and Vegetable Scramble 76

Duck and Blueberry Bites 77

Venison and Sweet Pea Mash 78

Pork and Apple Stew 79

Rabbit and Parsnip Puree 80

Special Treats: Healthy Snacks and Rewards
..81

Peanut Butter Pumpkin Treats 81

Sweet Potato Chews 82

Apple Crunch Pupcakes 83

Carrot and Banana Mini Muffins................84

Frozen Yogurt Pops.....................................84

Beefy Bites...85

Tuna Crackers..86

Chicken Jerky 87

Veggie Bones 87

Peanut Butter and Honey Ice Cream 88

14-day Puppy Meal Plans 90

Day 1-2: Introduction to Solid Food...........90

Day 3-4: Introducing Protein 90

Day 5-6: Incorporating Vegetables 91

Day 7-8: Introducing Variety 92

Day 9-10: Consistency and Routine.......... 92

Day 11-12: Solid Food Transition 93

Day 13-14: Establishing a Diet.................... 93

Health and Wellness 94

Foods to Boost Immunity and Overall Health 94

Managing Common Health Issues with Diet 98

Supplements: Do's and Don'ts 103

Common Supplements and Their Uses:.. 106

Conclusion 108

Chapter 1

INTRODUCTION

The Importance of a Balanced Diet for Dogs

A balanced diet is crucial for maintaining the health, energy, and longevity of dogs. Just like humans, dogs require a mix of proteins, carbohydrates, fats, vitamins, minerals, and water in specific proportions to function optimally. Each nutrient plays a vital role in the various bodily functions and contributes to the overall well-being of a canine.

Proteins are essential for growth, repair, and maintenance of body tissues. They are particularly important for puppies in their growth phase and for adult dogs to maintain their muscle mass. Carbohydrates provide energy, help in digestion, and can influence the health of the gut flora. Fats are a concentrated energy source, important for cell structure, and necessary for the absorption of certain vitamins.

Vitamins and minerals support immune function, bone health, and nerve signaling among other functions. They must be provided in the right amounts, as both deficiencies and excesses can lead to health problems. Water, often overlooked, is essential for hydration, digestion, and temperature regulation.

A balanced diet supports a healthy weight, reducing the risk of obesity and associated diseases like diabetes, heart disease, and joint problems. It also contributes to a strong immune system, reducing susceptibility to infections and illnesses. Moreover, a proper diet can influence a dog's coat and skin health, leading to a shiny coat and reducing skin disorders.

The specific dietary needs can vary based on a dog's age, breed, size, and activity level, as well as any special health considerations. Therefore, it's important to tailor the diet to the individual dog, sometimes with the guidance of a veterinarian or a canine nutritionist. Homemade diets, when done correctly, can provide all the necessary nutrients, but they require careful planning to avoid nutritional imbalances. Commercial dog foods are formulated to meet these nutritional standards, but quality can vary widely between brands.

Understanding Your Dog's Nutritional Needs

Understanding your dog's nutritional needs is fundamental to ensuring their health, vitality, and longevity. Dogs, like all animals, require a balanced blend of nutrients, each serving unique functions that contribute to their overall well-being. These nutritional requirements, however, are not one-size-fits-all and can vary significantly based on a dog's age, breed, weight, activity level, and health status.

At the core of a dog's diet are proteins, which are crucial for the growth and repair of tissues, and serve as building blocks for hormones and enzymes. Dogs need high-quality sources of protein for optimal health. The source of protein, whether from meat, fish, or legumes, should be easily digestible and appropriate for the dog's digestive system.

Fats are another essential component, providing energy, supporting cell function, and facilitating the absorption of fat-soluble vitamins. They also contribute to the health of a dog's skin and coat. However, the amount of fat must be balanced, as excessive fat can lead to obesity and related health issues.

Carbohydrates, while not technically essential, play a significant role in providing energy, supporting gut health, and aiding in digestion. They should come from sources that are easily digestible, with grains and vegetables being common ingredients in dog foods.

Vitamins and minerals are critical for various bodily functions, including bone development, vision, and blood clotting. Each vitamin and mineral has a specific role, and they must be supplied in the correct amounts to avoid deficiencies or toxicities.

Water is the most crucial nutrient, necessary for hydration, digestion, and temperature regulation. Ensuring that your dog has constant access to clean, fresh water is a simple yet vital aspect of their care.

Special dietary considerations may come into play for dogs with specific health issues, like allergies, sensitivities, or chronic conditions such as kidney disease or diabetes. In these cases, a veterinarian or a canine nutritionist might recommend a specialized diet to manage these health concerns effectively.

It's also important to recognize that a dog's nutritional needs change over their lifetime. Puppies have different requirements to support their rapid growth, adult dogs need a diet to maintain their health and energy levels, and senior dogs might need adjustments to accommodate decreased activity levels and metabolic changes.

Benefits of Homemade Dog Food

While there are many benefits to homemade dog food, it's important to approach this method with care. Ensuring that the diet is nutritionally balanced is crucial; deficiencies or excesses in nutrients can lead to health problems over time. Here are some key advantages of preparing homemade meals for dogs:

1. Control over Ingredients

Homemade dog food gives you complete control over what goes into your dog's diet. This is particularly beneficial for dogs with allergies, sensitivities, or specific dietary requirements. You can select high-quality, fresh ingredients, avoiding the fillers, preservatives, and artificial additives often found in commercial dog foods.

2. Tailored Nutrition

Every dog is unique, with their preferences, health issues, and nutritional needs. Homemade meals allow for the customization of recipes to suit your dog's age, size, activity level, and health status. This tailored approach can help manage weight, combat health issues, and ensure that your dog is receiving the optimal balance of nutrients.

3. Variety and Freshness

Just like humans, dogs enjoy variety in their diet. Homemade food can provide a diverse range of flavors and textures that can keep mealtime interesting for your dog. Using fresh ingredients also means that the food can be more nutrient-rich compared to some commercial options that may have been stored for long periods.

4. Stronger Bond

Preparing your dog's meals is an act of love and care. It can strengthen the bond between you and your pet, as you're directly involved in one of the most important aspects of their well-being. This hands-on approach to your dog's nutrition can also be more satisfying for you as a pet owner.

5. Potential Health Benefits

Many proponents of homemade dog food report seeing visible health benefits in their pets, including a shinier coat, healthier skin, more energy, and better overall health. The freshness of the ingredients and the absence of artificial additives may contribute to these improvements.

6. Economic Efficiency

While there's an assumption that homemade dog food is more expensive, it can be cost-effective depending on the ingredients used and how you source them. Buying ingredients in bulk, choosing seasonal produce, and using parts of meals prepared for human consumption can help manage costs.

7. Avoidance of Recalled Products

The pet food industry has seen its share of recalls due to contamination and safety issues. Preparing your dog's food at home can offer peace of mind by minimizing the risk associated with these recalls.

Chapter 2

Getting Started

Kitchen Essentials for Homemade Dog Food

Preparing homemade dog food requires not just the right ingredients but also a set of kitchen essentials that make the process efficient, safe, and enjoyable. Having the right tools can help ensure that the meals you prepare meet the nutritional needs of your dog while also saving you time and effort. Here are some kitchen essentials for anyone looking to prepare homemade dog food:

1. High-Quality Knife Set

A good set of sharp knives is essential for efficiently cutting, dicing, and chopping various ingredients such as meats, vegetables, and fruits.

2. Cutting Board

Having a dedicated cutting board for preparing your dog's meals helps maintain hygiene and prevent cross-contamination. Consider using color-coded cutting boards to keep things separate.

3. Measuring Cups and Spoons

Accuracy is key when it comes to adding ingredients to your dog's food, especially when following recipes designed to meet specific nutritional requirements. Measuring cups and spoons are indispensable for this purpose.

4. Food Processor or Blender

A food processor or blender can greatly simplify the preparation of homemade dog food, especially for making purees or blending ingredients to a consistency that's easy for your dog to eat and digest.

5. Large Mixing Bowls

Stainless steel or glass mixing bowls are perfect for combining ingredients. They're easy to clean, and having a few different sizes gives you flexibility depending on the quantity of food you're preparing.

6. Digital Scale

A digital kitchen scale is crucial for weighing ingredients, ensuring that your dog is getting the correct amounts of each nutrient. This is particularly important for maintaining a balanced diet.

7. Slow Cooker or Pressure Cooker

These appliances are excellent for cooking meats, vegetables, and grains at low temperatures, preserving nutrients while making the ingredients soft and easy to digest. They're also convenient for batch cooking.

8. Storage Containers

Once you've prepared your dog's food, you'll need a way to store it. BPA-free plastic containers or glass jars with airtight lids are perfect for keeping food fresh in the refrigerator or freezer.

9. Skimmer and Spatulas

A skimmer can help remove foam and fat from broths, ensuring a clearer, healthier liquid. Silicone spatulas are versatile tools for mixing ingredients and scraping bowls clean.

10. Parchment Paper or Silicone Mats

For baking homemade treats or dehydrating meats and vegetables, parchment paper or silicone baking mats can be very useful. They prevent sticking and ensure even cooking.

11. Oven and Stovetop

Essential for cooking, baking, and simmering ingredients. A reliable oven and stovetop are central to preparing a variety of meals.

12. Nutrition Guide or Cookbook

While not a kitchen tool, having a reliable source of recipes and nutritional guidelines is essential for ensuring the meals you prepare meet your dog's dietary needs.

Safe and Unsafe Ingredients for Dogs

When preparing homemade dog food, it's crucial to know which ingredients are safe and which can be harmful to your dog. Here's a guide to help you distinguish between the two, ensuring that your homemade meals contribute positively to your dog's health.

Safe Ingredients for Dogs

1. **Meats:** Cooked chicken, turkey, beef, and lamb are excellent protein sources. Remove all bones and avoid fatty cuts to prevent pancreatitis.

2. **Fish:** Cooked salmon and sardines are good for dogs, providing omega-3 fatty acids that support skin and coat health. Ensure all bones are removed.

3. **Vegetables:** Carrots, green beans, peas, and pumpkin can be given to dogs. They should be cooked without any added salt or seasonings and chopped to prevent choking.

4. **Fruits:** Apples (without seeds), bananas, blueberries, and watermelon (without seeds or rind) are safe and can be a healthy, low-calorie treat.

5. **Grains:** Rice, barley, and oatmeal can be good carbohydrate sources, especially for dogs with sensitive stomachs. Always cook grains thoroughly.

6. **Dairy:** Small amounts of plain yogurt or cottage cheese can be a good source of calcium and probiotics. Note that some dogs may be lactose intolerant.

Unsafe Ingredients for Dogs

1. **Onions and Garlic:** These can cause gastrointestinal irritation and could lead to red blood cell damage.

2. **Chocolate:** It contains theobromine, which is toxic to dogs and can lead to various health issues, including heart problems.

3. **Grapes and Raisins:** Even in small amounts, grapes and raisins can cause kidney failure in dogs.

4. **Avocado:** Persin, found in avocados, can cause vomiting and diarrhea in dogs.

5. **Xylitol:** This sweetener found in many sugar-free products can lead to liver failure and hypoglycemia.

6. **Alcohol and Caffeine:** These can cause a range of issues from vomiting and diarrhea to death.

7. **Macadamia Nuts:** These nuts can cause weakness, depression, vomiting, tremors, and hyperthermia.

8. **Bones:** Cooked bones can splinter and cause choking or serious damage to the dog's mouth, throat, or intestines.

9. **Raw Eggs, Meat, or Fish:** Raw diets are controversial due to the risk of bacterial infection like salmonella or E. coli, and certain raw fish can contain parasites.

How to Transition Your Dog to Homemade Meals

Transitioning your dog to homemade meals should be a gradual process to ensure it's easy on their digestive system and to gauge their acceptance of the new diet. Here's a step-by-step guide to making this transition smoothly and safely:

1. Consult with a Veterinarian

Before making any changes to your dog's diet, it's crucial to consult with a veterinarian. They can provide guidance tailored to your dog's specific health needs and nutritional requirements, ensuring the homemade diet is balanced and appropriate.

2. Research and Plan

Educate yourself on canine nutrition to understand the balance of proteins, fats, carbohydrates, vitamins, and minerals your dog needs. Plan meals that are complete and balanced, potentially with the help of a canine nutritionist or vet-approved resources.

3. Start with a Simple Recipe

Begin with a simple, vet-approved recipe that's suitable for your dog's dietary needs. Choose ingredients that your dog has eaten before to minimize the risk of allergic reactions.

4. Gradual Introduction

Start by mixing a small amount of the homemade food with their current food. A good rule of thumb is to start with about 10% homemade food and 90% commercial food. Gradually increase the homemade portion over 7-10 days, paying close attention to your dog's digestion and appetite.

5. Monitor Your Dog's Reaction

Observe your dog's reaction to the new diet. Look for signs of gastrointestinal distress such as vomiting, diarrhea, or constipation, as well as changes in energy levels and appetite. If any issues arise, consult your veterinarian.

6. Adjust Portions and Ingredients as Needed

As you transition, you may need to adjust the recipe or portion sizes based on your dog's energy levels, weight, and overall health. Homemade diets can require fine-tuning to get right.

7. Ensure Balanced Nutrition

A common pitfall with homemade diets is the potential for nutritional imbalances. Make sure the diet meets all your dog's nutritional needs. Supplements may be necessary to fill any gaps but only use them under veterinary guidance.

8. Establish a Routine

Once fully transitioned, establish a feeding routine with regular meal times. This helps with digestion and weight management.

9. Continued Monitoring and Adjustments

Even after successfully transitioning, continue to monitor your dog's health and adjust the diet as needed. Regular veterinary check-ups are important to ensure the homemade diet continues to meet your dog's nutritional needs over time.

10. Be Patient and Flexible

Every dog is different, and some may take longer to adjust to homemade food than others. Be patient and prepared to adjust your approach based on your dog's specific needs and preferences.

Chapter 3

Nutrition Basics

The Role of Proteins, Carbohydrates, and Fats

Proteins, carbohydrates, and fats play essential roles in both human and canine diets, serving as the primary sources of energy and supporting various bodily functions. Understanding the role of each nutrient can help in formulating a balanced diet that meets the nutritional needs of an individual or pet.

Proteins

Proteins are vital for the growth, repair, and maintenance of all body tissues. They are made up of amino acids, some of which are essential because the body cannot synthesize them. In dogs, proteins are crucial for:

- **Muscle Growth and Repair:** Proteins provide the building blocks for muscle development and help repair wear and tear in the body.
- **Immune Function:** Proteins are necessary for the production of antibodies and the healthy functioning of the immune system.
- **Hormones and Enzymes:** Many hormones and enzymes, that regulate various bodily functions, are proteins.
- **Energy:** While not the primary energy source, proteins can be used for energy if necessary.

High-quality protein sources for dogs include meat, fish, eggs, and some plants like legumes.

Carbohydrates

Carbohydrates provide a readily available source of energy. They are not considered essential in the diet of dogs, as they can meet their glucose needs through proteins and fats. However, carbohydrates can be part of a healthy diet for dogs, offering:

- **Energy:** Carbohydrates are broken down into glucose, the body's preferred energy source, especially for the brain and red blood cells.

- **Fiber:** Dietary fiber, a type of carbohydrate, supports digestive health by promoting regular bowel movements and aiding in the management of blood sugar levels.

- **Vitamins and Minerals:** Many carbohydrate sources, such as fruits and vegetables, are rich in vitamins and minerals that support overall health.

Good carbohydrate sources for dogs include vegetables, fruits, and whole grains, with an emphasis on those that provide dietary fiber.

Fats

Fats are the most concentrated form of energy in the diet and serve several important roles in the body, including:

- **Energy Storage:** Fats provide a reserve of energy, stored in the body's fat tissues.

- **Essential Fatty Acids:** Dogs require certain fatty acids that they cannot produce themselves, such as omega-3 and omega-6 fatty acids, which are important for skin and coat health, cell membrane integrity, and inflammation regulation.

- **Vitamin Absorption:** Fats help in the absorption of fat-soluble vitamins (A, D, E, and K) from the intestine.
- **Protection and Insulation:** Body fat acts as insulation to help regulate body temperature and provides cushioning to protect internal organs.

Healthy fat sources for dogs include fish oil, flaxseed, and the fats naturally found in meats.

Vitamins and Minerals: What Your Dog Needs

Vitamins and minerals play indispensable roles in the health and well-being of dogs, acting as essential components in various biological processes. These micronutrients support everything from bone health and nerve function to energy production and immune response. Unlike macronutrients such as proteins, fats, and carbohydrates, which are needed in larger quantities, vitamins and minerals are required in smaller amounts. However, their impact on a dog's health is profound.

Vitamins are organic compounds that dogs need to ingest in small quantities for proper health. They are crucial for maintaining normal metabolic functions, as they often act as coenzymes or parts of coenzymes, helping to facilitate the body's chemical reactions. For example, some vitamins are essential in converting the energy found in proteins, fats, and carbohydrates into ATP, the molecule that powers most of the body's cellular activities. Others play critical roles in blood clotting, wound healing, and maintaining healthy skin and bones.

Minerals, inorganic elements present in the soil and water, are absorbed by plants and ingested by animals. They are critical for the structural components of the body, such as bones and teeth, and are also essential for the transmission of nerve impulses, muscle contraction, and the maintenance of osmotic balance. Minerals are categorized into macrominerals, which are required in larger amounts, and trace minerals, needed in smaller quantities but are no less important for a dog's health and development.

The balance of vitamins and minerals is crucial; an excess or deficiency of these micronutrients can lead to health problems. For instance, an imbalance in certain minerals can affect a dog's bone growth, while a deficiency in certain vitamins can lead to skin issues, vision problems, and compromised immune function. This balance is not always easy to achieve, especially in homemade diets, which is why some dog owners opt for supplements. However, supplementation should be approached with caution and under veterinary guidance, as excessive supplementation can be just as harmful as a deficiency.

Given the complexity of nutritional science and the specific needs of individual dogs based on factors such as age, breed, and health status, formulating a diet that meets all of a dog's nutritional requirements can be challenging. This is where the advice of veterinary professionals becomes invaluable. They can guide diet formulation or recommend commercial diets that are formulated to meet the nutritional standards established by canine nutrition experts.

Hydration: Ensuring Your Dog Gets Enough Water

Hydration is as crucial for dogs as it is for humans, playing a vital role in maintaining overall health. Water facilitates countless bodily functions, including digestion, circulation, and waste removal. It helps regulate body temperature, lubricates joints, and aids in the absorption of nutrients. Ensuring your dog stays adequately hydrated is essential for their well-being, and understanding how to achieve this is key for any pet owner.

Dogs regulate their body temperature through panting, which evaporates moisture from their lungs and airways, and through sweating from the pads of their feet. Both processes consume a significant amount of water, making adequate hydration particularly crucial. The amount of water a dog needs can vary widely based on their size, diet, age, activity level, and the climate they live in. As a general rule, dogs should consume approximately one ounce of water per pound of body weight each day, but this can increase with exercise or hot weather.

Recognizing the signs of dehydration in dogs is vital. Symptoms can include lethargy, dry gums, excessive drooling, and sunken eyes. Severe dehydration can lead to critical issues such as kidney failure or heatstroke. Hence, monitoring your dog's water intake and ensuring they have constant access to clean, fresh water is fundamental.

Feeding your dog a diet that includes wet food can also help maintain hydration, as wet food has a high moisture content. However, this doesn't negate the need for fresh water. Some dogs, especially those on dry food diets, may require more encouragement to drink enough water. This can include providing multiple water bowls around the house, considering the use of pet water fountains that keep water circulating and appealing, and even flavoring the water with a bit of chicken broth to make it more enticing.

Activity and weather also play significant roles in a dog's hydration needs. Dogs that are more active or live in hot climates will need more water. It's important to bring water for your dog on long walks or any outdoor activity, offering it regularly, especially in warm weather to prevent overheating and dehydration.

Regularly cleaning your dog's water bowl is also important to prevent the buildup of bacteria and encourage them to drink more frequently. A clean bowl is more inviting and ensures the water tastes fresh.

Incorporating hydration checks into your daily routine can help keep your dog healthy. You can check for dehydration by gently lifting the skin on the back of your dog's neck or between the shoulder blades. If the skin snaps back into place immediately, they are likely well-hydrated. If it takes a moment to fall back into place, your dog may be dehydrated.

In conclusion, maintaining proper hydration is a simple yet critical aspect of caring for your dog. It supports their health in myriad ways, from digestion and nutrient absorption to temperature regulation and joint lubrication. By ensuring your dog has constant access to clean water, monitoring their intake, and understanding the signs of dehydration, you can help keep them healthy and happy.

Chapter 4

Simple Starters Easy Recipes for Beginners

Chicken and Rice Delight

Ingredients:

- 1 cup cooked chicken, shredded
- 1 cup cooked brown rice
- 1/2 cup steamed carrots, diced
- 1 tablespoon olive oil

Instructions:

1. Mix the cooked chicken, brown rice, and steamed carrots in a bowl.
2. Drizzle with olive oil and stir to combine.

Nutritional Info: Rich in protein from chicken, complex carbohydrates from brown rice, and beta-carotene from carrots. Olive oil provides essential fatty acids.

Beefy Veggie Mix

Ingredients:

- 1 cup cooked lean ground beef, drained
- 1 cup boiled potatoes, diced
- 1/2 cup green beans, chopped and steamed
- 1 teaspoon flaxseed oil

Instructions:

1. Combine the cooked beef, boiled potatoes, and green beans in a bowl.
2. Add flaxseed oil and mix well.

Nutritional Info: Lean beef offers high-quality protein and iron, potatoes provide potassium and carbohydrates, green beans add fiber, and flaxseed oil is a good source of omega-3 fatty acids.

Turkey and Pea Pod Pottage

Ingredients:

- 1 cup cooked turkey, chopped
- 1 cup cooked quinoa
- 1/2 cup peas
- 1 tablespoon pumpkin puree

Instructions:

1. Mix the cooked turkey, quinoa, and peas.
2. Stir in the pumpkin puree for added fiber and moisture.

Nutritional Info: Turkey is a lean protein, quinoa is a gluten-free carbohydrate with amino acids, peas provide fiber and vitamins, and pumpkin is rich in fiber and vitamin A.

Salmon Sweet Potato Hash

Ingredients:

- 1 cup cooked, deboned salmon

- 1 cup baked sweet potato, mashed
- 1/4 cup chopped spinach
- 1 teaspoon coconut oil

Instructions:

1. Combine salmon, sweet potato, and spinach in a bowl.
2. Mix in coconut oil for healthy fats.

Nutritional Info: Salmon contains omega-3 fatty acids, sweet potato is a source of beta-carotene and complex carbs, spinach provides iron and calcium, and coconut oil supports skin and coat health.

Simple Chicken Broth Soup

Ingredients:

- 1 cup shredded chicken
- 2 cups low-sodium chicken broth
- 1/2 cup cooked oatmeal
- 1/4 cup peas

Instructions:

1. In a pot, combine all ingredients and simmer for 10 minutes.
2. Allow cooling before serving.

Nutritional Info: Provides hydration, protein from chicken, fiber from oatmeal, and vitamins from peas.

Easy Egg and Potato Scramble

Ingredients:

- 2 eggs, scrambled
- 1 boiled potato, diced
- 1/4 cup cottage cheese

Instructions:

1. Mix scrambled eggs and boiled potato.
2. Stir in cottage cheese before serving.

Nutritional Info: Eggs are a complete protein source, potatoes offer carbohydrates and vitamin C, and cottage cheese adds calcium.

Puppy Pumpkin Rice

Ingredients:

- 1 cup cooked brown rice
- 1/2 cup canned pumpkin (not pie filling)
- 1/4 cup shredded turkey

Instructions:

1. Combine all ingredients in a bowl and mix well.

Nutritional Info: High in fiber from pumpkin, protein from turkey, and carbohydrates from rice.

Veggie Beef Bliss

Ingredients:

- 1 cup cooked lean ground beef
- 1/2 cup cooked barley

- 1/2 cup steamed broccoli, chopped
- 1 teaspoon olive oil

Instructions:

1. Mix beef, barley, and broccoli.
2. Drizzle with olive oil before serving.

Nutritional Info: Beef for protein, barley for fiber and vitamins, broccoli for antioxidants, and olive oil for healthy fats.

Fisherman's Feast

Ingredients:

- 1 cup cooked, deboned white fish
- 1/2 cup cooked peas
- 1/2 cup cooked carrots, diced
- 1 tablespoon parsley, chopped

Instructions:

1. Flake the fish and mix it with peas and carrots.
2. Garnish with parsley before serving.

Nutritional Info: Fish provides lean protein and omega-3 fatty acids, peas and carrots offer vitamins and fiber, and parsley can help freshen breath.

Canine Cottage Pie

Ingredients:

- 1 cup cooked lean ground turkey
- 1 cup mashed cauliflower
- 1/4 cup green beans, chopped
- 1 teaspoon turmeric

Instructions:

1. Layer the ground turkey and green beans in a bowl.
2. Top with mashed cauliflower and sprinkle with turmeric.

Nutritional Info: Turkey is a source of lean protein, cauliflower is low in carbs and high in vitamins, green beans add fiber, and turmeric has anti-inflammatory properties.

Chapter 5

Protein Power: Meat, Fish, and Egg Recipes

Classic Beef Stew

Ingredients:

- 1 pound lean beef, cubed
- 2 carrots, sliced
- 1 sweet potato, cubed
- 1/2 cup peas
- Water

Instructions:

1. In a large pot, cover the beef with water and simmer until tender.
2. Add carrots and sweet potato; cook until soft.
3. Stir in peas and cook for an additional 5 minutes.

Nutritional Info: Lean beef is rich in protein and iron, carrots and sweet potatoes are high in fiber and beta-carotene, and peas provide vitamins and minerals.

Chicken & Quinoa Dinner

Ingredients:

- 1 chicken breast, cooked and shredded
- 1 cup quinoa, cooked
- 1/2 cup spinach, chopped
- 1 tablespoon olive oil

Instructions:

1. Mix shredded chicken, cooked quinoa, and spinach.
2. Drizzle with olive oil before serving.

Nutritional Info: Chicken is an excellent protein source, quinoa is a complete protein grain, spinach offers vitamins A, C, and K, and olive oil provides healthy fats.

Salmon Rice Bowl

Ingredients:

- 1 salmon fillet, cooked and deboned
- 1 cup brown rice, cooked
- 1/4 cup zucchini, finely chopped
- 1 teaspoon flaxseed oil

Instructions:

1. Flake the salmon and mix it with cooked brown rice and zucchini.
2. Add flaxseed oil and combine well.

Nutritional Info: Salmon is high in omega-3 fatty acids, brown rice is a good source of carbohydrates, zucchini is rich in vitamins, and flaxseed oil promotes a healthy coat.

Turkey and Vegetable Loaf

Ingredients:

- 1 pound ground turkey
- 1 egg
- 1/2 cup carrots, grated

- 1/2 cup apples, grated
- 1 cup rolled oats

Instructions:

1. Preheat oven to 350°F (175°C).
2. Mix all ingredients in a bowl and press into a loaf pan.
3. Bake for 45 minutes.

Nutritional Info: Turkey is a lean protein, eggs provide biotin and vitamin B, carrots and apples offer fiber and vitamins, and oats are a good source of energy.

Beefy Pumpkin Mash

Ingredients:

- 1 pound lean ground beef
- 1 cup pumpkin puree (not pie filling)
- 1/4 cup peas
- 1/4 cup carrots, diced

Instructions:

1. Cook beef over medium heat until browned.
2. Mix in pumpkin puree, peas, and carrots, cooking until vegetables are tender.

Nutritional Info: Beef is a high-quality protein, pumpkin is high in fiber and vitamin A, and peas and carrots provide additional nutrients and antioxidants.

Egg & Veggie Scramble

Ingredients:

- 2 eggs, beaten
- 1/4 cup spinach, chopped
- 1/4 cup zucchini, chopped
- 1 tablespoon coconut oil

Instructions:

1. Heat coconut oil in a pan.
2. Add vegetables, cooking until soft.

3. Pour in eggs and scramble until cooked.

Nutritional Info: Eggs are a complete protein, spinach, and zucchini are rich in vitamins and minerals, and coconut oil supports skin and coat health.

Sardine Delight

Ingredients:

- 1 can of sardines in water, drained
- 1/2 cup cooked oatmeal
- 1/4 cup carrots, shredded
- 1/4 cup peas

Instructions:

1. Mix sardines, oatmeal, carrots, and peas in a bowl.

Nutritional Info: Sardines are an excellent source of omega-3 fatty acids and protein, oatmeal provides fiber, carrots, and peas add vitamins and minerals.

Liver and Lentil Stew

Ingredients:

- 1/2 pound beef liver, chopped
- 1 cup lentils, cooked
- 1 carrot, diced
- Water

Instructions:

1. Simmer liver and carrot in water until the liver is cooked through.
2. Add cooked lentils and heat through.

Nutritional Info: The liver is rich in vitamins A and B, lentils provide plant-based protein and fiber, and carrots add beta-carotene and vitamins.

Chicken and Egg Breakfast Patties

Ingredients:

- 1 chicken breast, cooked and shredded
- 2 eggs, beaten

- 1/4 cup rolled oats
- 1 tablespoon parsley, chopped

Instructions:

1. Combine all ingredients and form into small patties.
2. Cook in a lightly oiled pan until each side is golden brown.

Nutritional Info: Provides high-quality protein from chicken and eggs, oats for fiber, and parsley for fresh breath and vitamins.

Tuna and Sweet Potato Balls

Ingredients:

- 1 can tuna in water, drained
- 1 sweet potato, cooked and mashed
- 1 egg, beaten
- 1/2 cup breadcrumbs or rolled oats

Instructions:

1. Mix tuna, sweet potato, and egg.

2. Form into balls, coat with breadcrumbs or oats, and bake at 350°F (175°C) for 20 minutes.

Nutritional Info: Tuna is a great source of omega-3 fatty acids and protein, sweet potatoes are rich in beta-carotene, and oats/breadcrumbs add fiber.

Chapter 6

Vegetarian Options for Dogs

Sweet Potato and Lentil Loaf

Ingredients:

- 2 cups cooked lentils
- 1 large sweet potato, cooked and mashed
- 1 cup rolled oats
- 1/4 cup carrot, grated
- 2 tablespoons olive oil
- 1 teaspoon turmeric

Instructions:

1. Preheat the oven to 375°F (190°C).
2. Mix all ingredients in a large bowl.
3. Press the mixture into a loaf pan.
4. Bake for 40 minutes.

Nutritional Info: Lentils and oats provide plant-based protein and fiber, sweet potato is rich in beta-carotene, and turmeric offers anti-inflammatory benefits.

Quinoa Veggie Patties

Ingredients:

- 1 cup cooked quinoa
- 1/2 cup peas
- 1/2 cup grated zucchini
- 1 egg (or flaxseed egg for a vegan option)
- 1 tablespoon coconut oil

Instructions:

1. Mix quinoa, peas, zucchini, and egg in a bowl.
2. Form into small patties.
3. Fry in coconut oil until golden on both sides.

Nutritional Info: Quinoa provides complete protein, peas are rich in vitamins, zucchini offers dietary fiber, and coconut oil is good for the coat.

Pumpkin Rice Pudding

Ingredients:

- 1 cup cooked brown rice
- 1/2 cup pumpkin puree
- 1/4 cup coconut milk
- 1 teaspoon cinnamon

Instructions:

1. Mix all ingredients in a pot.
2. Simmer on low heat for 10 minutes, stirring frequently.

Nutritional Info: Brown rice is a source of carbohydrates, pumpkin is high in fiber and vitamin A, coconut milk provides healthy fats, and cinnamon has anti-inflammatory properties.

Tofu and Vegetable Stir-fry

Ingredients:

- 1 cup firm tofu, cubed
- 1 cup broccoli, chopped
- 1/2 cup carrots, sliced
- 2 tablespoons sesame oil
- 1 teaspoon ginger, minced

Instructions:

1. Heat sesame oil in a pan.
2. Add ginger, tofu, and vegetables.
3. Stir-fry until vegetables are tender but crisp.

Nutritional Info: Tofu is a great source of protein, broccoli and carrots offer vitamins and minerals, sesame oil provides healthy fats, and ginger aids digestion.

Peanut Butter Oatmeal Cookies

Ingredients:

- 2 cups rolled oats
- 1/2 cup natural peanut butter (xylitol-free)
- 1 banana, mashed
- 1/4 cup water

Instructions:

1. Preheat the oven to 350°F (175°C).
2. Mix all ingredients to form a dough.
3. Drop spoonfuls onto a baking sheet and flatten.
4. Bake for 15 minutes.

Nutritional Info: Oats are high in fiber, peanut butter provides healthy fats and protein, and banana offers potassium and carbohydrates.

Veggie Doggie Chili

Ingredients:

- 1 cup kidney beans, cooked
- 1 cup diced tomatoes
- 1/2 cup corn
- 1/2 cup quinoa, cooked
- 1 teaspoon cumin

Instructions:

1. Combine all ingredients in a pot.
2. Simmer for 20 minutes, stirring occasionally.

Nutritional Info: Kidney beans and quinoa provide plant-based protein, tomatoes and corn are rich in vitamins and minerals, and cumin aids digestion.

Cheesy Veggie Muffins

Ingredients:

- 1 cup whole wheat flour

- 1/2 cup grated cheese (choose a low-fat option)
- 1/4 cup applesauce
- 1/4 cup shredded carrots
- 1 egg

Instructions:

1. Preheat the oven to 350°F (175°C).
2. Mix all ingredients in a bowl.
3. Spoon into muffin tins.
4. Bake for 20 minutes.

Nutritional Info: Whole wheat flour offers fiber, cheese provides calcium and protein, applesauce adds natural sweetness, and carrots are high in beta-carotene.

Spinach and Cottage Cheese Balls

Ingredients:

- 1 cup spinach, cooked and chopped
- 1/2 cup cottage cheese

- 1/4 cup breadcrumbs
- 1 egg

Instructions:

1. Mix all ingredients in a bowl.
2. Form into balls and place on a greased baking sheet.
3. Bake at 350°F (175°C) for 20 minutes.

Nutritional Info: Spinach is rich in iron and vitamins, cottage cheese offers protein and calcium, and breadcrumbs add texture and carbohydrates.

Sweet Pea and Carrot Mash

Ingredients:

- 1 cup peas, cooked
- 1 cup carrots, cooked and mashed
- 1 tablespoon olive oil
- 1 teaspoon dried mint

Instructions:

1. Blend peas and carrots.

2. Mix in olive oil and mint.

Nutritional Info: Peas provide protein and vitamins, carrots are a source of beta-carotene, olive oil is good for the skin and coat, and mint supports digestion.

Butternut Squash and Apple Puree

Ingredients:

- 1 cup butternut squash, cooked and mashed
- 1 apple, cooked and pureed
- 1 teaspoon flaxseed oil

Instructions:

1. Mix butternut squash and apple.
2. Stir in flaxseed oil.

Nutritional Info: Butternut squash is high in vitamins A and C, apple provides fiber and antioxidants, and flaxseed oil is a source of omega-3 fatty acids.

Chapter 7

Grain-Free Meals for Sensitive Stomachs

Chicken and Sweet Potato Stew

Ingredients:

- 1 pound chicken breast, cubed

- 2 sweet potatoes, peeled and cubed

- 1 carrot, sliced

- 4 cups chicken broth (make sure it's low-sodium and onion-free)

Instructions:

1. Combine all ingredients in a large pot.

2. Bring to a boil, then simmer until the chicken is cooked through and vegetables are tender.

Nutritional Info: Chicken provides lean protein, sweet potatoes are a rich source of beta-carotene and fiber, and carrots add vitamins and minerals.

Beef and Pumpkin Dinner

Ingredients:

- 1 pound lean ground beef
- 1 cup canned pumpkin (not pie filling)
- 1/2 cup peas
- 1/4 cup carrots, finely chopped

Instructions:

1. Brown the ground beef in a pan and drain the fat.

2. Mix beef with pumpkin, peas, and carrots.

3. Cook on low heat for 10 minutes.

Nutritional Info: Beef offers high-quality protein, pumpkin is high in fiber and good for digestion, and peas and carrots provide vitamins.

Salmon and Zucchini Hash

Ingredients:

- 1 salmon fillet, cooked and flaked
- 1 cup zucchini, diced
- 1 tablespoon coconut oil
- 1/4 teaspoon dried dill

Instructions:

1. In a pan, heat coconut oil over medium heat.
2. Add zucchini and cook until tender.
3. Mix in salmon and dill, and cook for an additional 5 minutes.

Nutritional Info: Salmon is rich in omega-3 fatty acids, zucchini is low in calories and high in vitamins, and coconut oil is beneficial for the coat.

Turkey and Carrot Patties

Ingredients:

- 1 pound ground turkey
- 1 cup carrots, grated
- 1 egg, beaten
- 1 tablespoon olive oil

Instructions:

1. Mix ground turkey, grated carrots, and egg.
2. Form into patties.
3. Fry in olive oil until fully cooked.

Nutritional Info: Turkey is a lean protein source, carrots provide dietary fiber and antioxidants, and olive oil contains healthy fats.

Lamb and Pea Puree

Ingredients:

- 1 pound lamb, cooked and chopped
- 1 cup peas, cooked
- 1 tablespoon parsley, chopped
- Water, as needed for blending

Instructions:

1. Blend lamb, peas, and parsley with enough water to make a puree.
2. Serve chilled or at room temperature.

Nutritional Info: Lamb is rich in protein and essential amino acids, peas are a good source of vitamins K and C, and parsley can help freshen breath.

Egg and Vegetable Scramble

Ingredients:

- 2 eggs
- 1/2 cup spinach, chopped
- 1/4 cup bell peppers, diced
- 1 tablespoon coconut oil

Instructions:

1. Beat the eggs in a bowl.
2. Heat coconut oil in a pan, add vegetables, and sauté until soft.
3. Add eggs and scramble until cooked.

Nutritional Info: Eggs provide high-quality protein and essential vitamins, spinach offers iron, and bell peppers are rich in vitamins A and C.

Duck and Blueberry Bites

Ingredients:

- 1 pound duck breast, cooked and diced

- 1 cup blueberries

- 1/2 cup carrots, grated

- 1 tablespoon flaxseed meal

Instructions:

1. Mix duck, blueberries, carrots, and flaxseed meal.

2. Serve in small portions.

Nutritional Info: Duck is a novel protein for many dogs, blueberries are high in antioxidants, carrots provide beta-carotene, and flaxseed meal offers omega-3 fatty acids.

Venison and Sweet Pea Mash

Ingredients:

- 1 pound venison, cooked and minced

- 1 cup sweet peas, cooked

- 1 tablespoon mint, finely chopped

- 1/4 cup sweet potato, cooked and mashed

Instructions:

1. Combine venison, sweet peas, mint, and sweet potato.

2. Mash together until well blended.

Nutritional Info: Venison is a lean protein source, sweet peas, and sweet potatoes are rich in fiber and nutrients, and mint supports digestion.

Pork and Apple Stew

Ingredients:

- 1 pound pork loin, cubed

- 2 apples, peeled and cubed

- 1/2 cup green beans, chopped

- 4 cups water

Instructions:

1. Combine all ingredients in a pot.

2. Simmer until pork is tender and vegetables are cooked.

Nutritional Info: Pork offers a high-quality protein, apples provide fiber and vitamins, and green beans are rich in vitamins A, C, and K.

Rabbit and Parsnip Puree

Ingredients:

- 1 pound rabbit, cooked and chopped

- 1 cup parsnips, cooked and mashed

- 1/4 cup parsley, chopped

- Water, as needed for blending

Instructions:

1. Blend rabbit, parsnips, and parsley with enough water to achieve a pureed consistency.

Nutritional Info: Rabbit is a high-protein, low-fat meat, parsnips are a good source of fiber and potassium, and parsley can help with bad breath.

Chapter 8

Special Treats: Healthy Snacks and Rewards

Peanut Butter Pumpkin Treats

Ingredients:

- 2 cups whole wheat flour (or any dog-safe alternative)
- 1/2 cup canned pumpkin (not pie filling)
- 1/4 cup natural peanut butter (xylitol-free)
- 2 eggs

Instructions:

1. Preheat your oven to 350°F (175°C).
2. Mix all ingredients in a bowl until a dough forms.
3. Roll out the dough and cut into shapes with a cookie cutter.
4. Bake for 20-25 minutes until hard.

Nutritional Info: Pumpkin is high in fiber and good for digestion, peanut butter provides healthy fats and proteins, and eggs are a great protein source.

Sweet Potato Chews

Ingredients:

- 1 large sweet potato, washed and dried

Instructions:

1. Preheat your oven to 250°F (120°C).
2. Cut the sweet potato into thin slices, about 1/4 inch thick.
3. Place on a baking sheet lined with parchment paper.
4. Bake for 2-3 hours, flipping halfway through, until they are dry and chewy.

Nutritional Info: Sweet potatoes are a great source of beta-carotene, vitamins, and fiber, making them an excellent low-fat treat.

Apple Crunch Pupcakes

Ingredients:

- 2 cups water
- 1/4 cup unsweetened applesauce
- 2 cups whole wheat flour
- 1 tsp baking powder
- 1/2 cup grated apple

Instructions:

1. Preheat your oven to 350°F (175°C).
2. Mix all ingredients until well combined.
3. Pour into mini muffin tins.
4. Bake for 25 minutes.

Nutritional Info: Apples provide fiber and vitamins, while applesauce adds natural sweetness without added sugar.

Carrot and Banana Mini Muffins

Ingredients:

- 1 banana, mashed
- 1 carrot, grated
- 1 egg
- 1 cup whole wheat flour
- 1 tsp baking powder

Instructions:

1. Preheat your oven to 350°F (175°C).
2. Combine all ingredients in a bowl.
3. Spoon into mini muffin pans.
4. Bake for 15-20 minutes.

Nutritional Info: Bananas are a good source of potassium and carbohydrates, and carrots provide beta-carotene and fiber.

Frozen Yogurt Pops

Ingredients:

- 1 cup plain, unsweetened yogurt
- 1/2 cup fresh blueberries

- 1 tablespoon honey (optional)

Instructions:

1. Mix yogurt, blueberries, and honey in a bowl.
2. Pour into ice cube trays or small cups.
3. Freeze until solid.

Nutritional Info: Yogurt provides calcium and probiotics, and blueberries are rich in antioxidants.

Beefy Bites

Ingredients:

- 1/2 pound lean ground beef
- 1/4 cup grated carrot
- 1/4 cup grated zucchini
- 1 egg

Instructions:

1. Preheat your oven to 350°F (175°C).
2. Mix all ingredients and form into small balls.

3. Place on a baking sheet and bake for 15 minutes.

Nutritional Info: Lean beef is a great source of protein and iron, while carrots and zucchini add vitamins, minerals, and fiber.

Tuna Crackers

Ingredients:

- 1 can tuna in water, drained
- 1 cup whole wheat flour
- 1 egg

Instructions:

1. Preheat your oven to 350°F (175°C).
2. Mix all ingredients to form a dough.
3. Roll out the dough and cut into small shapes.
4. Bake for 20 minutes.

Nutritional Info: Tuna provides omega-3 fatty acids and proteins, making these crackers a heart-healthy treat.

Chicken Jerky

Ingredients:

- 2 chicken breasts

Instructions:

1. Preheat your oven to 200°F (93°C).
2. Thinly slice chicken breasts.
3. Place slices on a baking sheet lined with parchment paper.
4. Bake for 2 hours or until the slices are dry and hard.

Nutritional Info: Chicken is a lean protein that's perfect for muscle health and energy.

Veggie Bones

Ingredients:

- 1/2 cup pureed pumpkin
- 1/4 cup water
- 2 cups whole wheat flour
- 1/2 cup oats
- 1/4 cup grated carrots

Instructions:

1. Preheat your oven to 350°F (175°C).
2. Mix all ingredients to form a stiff dough.
3. Roll out and cut into bone shapes.
4. Bake for 30-35 minutes.

Nutritional Info: Pumpkins and carrots are great for digestion, and oats add fiber and nutrients.

Peanut Butter and Honey Ice Cream

Ingredients:

- 2 bananas, sliced and frozen
- 2 tablespoons natural peanut butter
- 2 tablespoons honey

Instructions:

1. Blend frozen bananas in a food processor until smooth.
2. Add peanut butter and honey, and blend until mixed.

3. Freeze until solid.

Nutritional Info: Bananas offer potassium and fiber, peanut butter provides healthy fats and proteins, and honey adds a touch of natural sweetness.

Chapter 9

14-day Puppy Meal Plans

Day 1-2: Introduction to Solid Food

- **Breakfast:** Puppy kibble moistened with warm water or puppy milk replacer.

- **Lunch:** A small portion of pureed pumpkin mixed with puppy kibble.

- **Dinner:** Puppy kibble softened with warm chicken broth (ensure no onions or garlic in the broth).

Day 3-4: Introducing Protein

- **Breakfast:** Softened puppy kibble with a small spoon of plain, unsweetened yogurt.

- **Lunch:** Boiled chicken (no bones or skin) finely shredded, mixed into the softened kibble.

- **Dinner:** Softened puppy kibble; consider adding a teaspoon of cottage cheese.

Day 5-6: Incorporating Vegetables

- **Breakfast:** Puppy kibble with finely grated carrot mixed in.

- **Lunch:** A small portion of mashed sweet potato mixed with boiled chicken and kibble.

- **Dinner:** Softened kibble with a little boiled egg (fully cooked) crumbled in.

Day 7-8: Introducing Variety

- **Breakfast:** Softened kibble with a small amount of salmon (cooked and deboned) for omega-3s.

- **Lunch:** Kibble with finely chopped, steamed green beans.

- **Dinner:** Softened kibble mixed with a small portion of ground turkey, cooked thoroughly.

Day 9-10: Consistency and Routine

- **Breakfast:** Continue with kibble and a teaspoon of plain yogurt.

- **Lunch:** Kibble mixed with a small serving of cottage cheese and shredded chicken.

- **Dinner:** Softened kibble with boiled egg and mashed sweet potato.

Day 11-12: Solid Food Transition

- **Breakfast:** Kibble slightly less softened, with a bit of pureed pumpkin.

- **Lunch:** Kibble with a small amount of cooked, deboned fish.

- **Dinner:** Less softened kibble mixed with finely grated carrot and boiled chicken.

Day 13-14: Establishing a Diet

- **Breakfast:** Regular puppy kibble with a spoon of unsweetened yogurt.

- **Lunch:** Kibble with boiled or steamed vegetables (carrots, peas).

- **Dinner:** Kibble mixed with a small portion of cooked meat (chicken, beef, or turkey).

Health and Wellness

Foods to Boost Immunity and Overall Health

1. Lean Proteins

- **Chicken, Turkey, and Beef:** High-quality, cooked, lean meats are excellent sources of protein, essential for muscle repair and growth.
- **Fish:** Salmon, sardines, and mackerel are rich in omega-3 fatty acids, which support skin, coat, and cognitive health.

2. Fruits

- **Blueberries:** Packed with antioxidants, blueberries can help combat free radicals and support cellular health.

- **Apples (without seeds):** Provide fiber, and vitamins A and C; always remove the core and seeds.
- **Bananas:** A good source of potassium and carbohydrates for energy.

3. Vegetables

- **Carrots:** Rich in beta-carotene for vision health and a good source of fiber.
- **Sweet Potatoes:** High in beta-carotene and vitamins A and C, supporting the immune system.
- **Pumpkin:** Great for digestion due to its high fiber content; ensure it's pure pumpkin, not pie filling.

4. Whole Grains (For Dogs Without Grain Allergies)

- **Brown Rice and Oatmeal:** Provide carbohydrates for energy and are good sources of fiber, vitamins, and minerals.

5. Dairy (In Moderation)

- **Plain Yogurt:** Contains probiotics that can help maintain the balance of good bacteria in the gut.
- **Cottage Cheese:** A good source of calcium and protein, but only in small amounts due to lactose.

6. Healthy Fats

- **Flaxseeds and Chia Seeds:** Rich in omega-3 fatty acids, which can reduce inflammation and support brain health.
- **Coconut Oil:** Contains medium-chain triglycerides, known for their antimicrobial and antifungal properties.

7. Eggs

- **Whole Eggs:** Offer highly digestible protein, and are rich in selenium and vitamin B12, supporting the immune system and energy metabolism.

8. Leafy Greens

- **Spinach and Kale:** High in antioxidants, vitamins A, C, E, and K, and contain iron and calcium.

9. Broccoli

- Contains vitamins C and K, fiber, and antioxidants, but should be given in very small quantities due to its isothiocyanates content, which can cause gastric irritation in larger amounts.

10. Algae

- **Spirulina:** A superfood algae, rich in antioxidants, vitamins, and minerals, known for its immune-boosting properties.

Managing Common Health Issues with Diet

Diet plays a crucial role in managing common health issues in dogs. By adjusting what your dog eats, you can alleviate symptoms, prevent flare-ups, and sometimes even address the root cause of health problems. Here's how diet can help manage some common canine health issues, but remember, any dietary changes should be discussed with and monitored by a veterinarian.

Obesity

- **Dietary Management:** Focus on low-calorie, high-fiber diets to promote satiety and weight loss. Incorporate lean proteins and vegetables while reducing fat and carbohydrate intake.

- **Specific Foods:** Green beans, pumpkin, and lean meats like chicken or turkey can replace higher-calorie foods without leaving your dog feeling hungry.

Diabetes

- **Dietary Management:** Consistent, moderate to low carbohydrate diets help regulate blood sugar levels. High-fiber diets are also beneficial as they can slow glucose absorption.

- **Specific Foods:** Foods with a low glycemic index, like non-starchy vegetables (e.g., broccoli, green beans) and complex carbohydrates like barley and oats, can be beneficial.

Allergies

- **Dietary Management:** Identifying and eliminating allergens is key. This often involves a trial and error process with limited ingredient diets (LID) or hypoallergenic diets formulated to minimize the risk of allergic reactions.

- **Specific Foods:** Novel proteins (proteins your dog has never eaten) and hydrolyzed diets (where the protein is broken down so the immune system doesn't recognize it as an allergen) can be effective.

Kidney Disease

- **Dietary Management:** Low-protein, low-phosphorus, and high-moisture diets can help manage kidney disease by reducing the workload on the kidneys.

- **Specific Foods:** Foods high in omega-3 fatty acids, like fish oil, can help reduce inflammation. Non-dairy sources of calcium can also bind phosphates, reducing their absorption.

Digestive Issues

- **Dietary Management:** Highly digestible diets with soluble and insoluble fiber can support digestive health. Probiotics may also be beneficial for maintaining a healthy gut flora.
- **Specific Foods:** Easily digestible carbohydrates (like rice and sweet potatoes), lean meats, and pumpkin can soothe the digestive tract.

Arthritis and Joint Health

- **Dietary Management:** Diets high in omega-3 fatty acids and antioxidants can help reduce inflammation and support joint health.

- **Specific Foods:** Fish oil, chia seeds, and foods rich in vitamins E and C, like blueberries and spinach, can support joint health.

Heart Disease

- **Dietary Management:** Low-sodium diets are often recommended to manage heart disease, along with balanced levels of omega-3 fatty acids to support heart health.

- **Specific Foods:** Foods low in sodium and high in omega-3s, like flaxseeds and fish, are beneficial. Taurine, found in meat, is also important for heart health.

Liver Disease

- **Dietary Management:** Diets low in copper and rich in highly digestible proteins can help manage liver conditions. Antioxidants can also support liver health.

- **Specific Foods:** White fish, chicken, and eggs provide high-quality protein. Vegetables like broccoli and spinach offer antioxidants without overloading the liver.

Supplements: Do's and Don'ts

Supplementing your dog's diet can offer numerous health benefits, from improving coat quality to supporting joint health. However, it's crucial to approach supplementation with care to avoid potential pitfalls.

Here are some guidelines on the dos and don'ts when considering supplements for your dog.

Do's

1. **Do Consult Your Veterinarian**

Always consult with a veterinarian before starting any supplement. They can advise whether a supplement is necessary based on your dog's health, diet, and specific needs.

2. **Do Research Quality Brands**

Look for reputable brands that have conducted clinical trials or have their products tested by third parties. Quality and sourcing are crucial for efficacy and safety.

3. **Do Follow the Recommended Dosages**

Stick to the recommended dosages based on your dog's weight and health status. More is not always better and can sometimes lead to adverse effects.

4. **Do Consider Your Dog's Diet**

Assess your dog's current diet to determine if there are nutritional gaps that need to be filled. Some commercial dog foods are already nutritionally complete and may only require supplements for specific health issues.

5. **Do Introduce Supplements Gradually**

When starting a new supplement, introduce it gradually to monitor for any adverse reactions or sensitivities.

Don'ts

1. **Don't Assume Human Supplements Are Safe for Dogs**

Many supplements designed for humans contain ingredients that are harmful to dogs. Never give human supplements to your dog without veterinary approval.

2. **Don't Over-Supplement**

Adding too many supplements can lead to nutritional imbalances and health issues. More is not always better.

3. **Don't Use Supplements to Replace Medicine**

Supplements can support health but should not replace prescribed medications for treating diseases unless advised by your veterinarian.

4. **Don't Ignore Side Effects**

If you notice any adverse reactions after starting a supplement, stop administration and consult your veterinarian immediately.

5. **Don't Mix Supplements Without Approval**

Some supplements can interact with each other or with medications. Discuss with your vet any supplements you're considering giving simultaneously.

Common Supplements and Their Uses:

- **Omega-3 Fatty Acids:** Support skin and coat health, reduce inflammation, and can benefit heart and joint health.

- **Glucosamine and Chondroitin:** Often used for joint health and to alleviate symptoms of arthritis.

- **Probiotics:** Support digestive health and aid in maintaining a healthy gut flora.

- **Antioxidants (Vitamins A, C, and E):** Can improve immune function and help reduce the effects of aging.

Chapter 10

Conclusion

As we close the pages of this journey through nutrition and culinary exploration for our beloved dogs, it's important to reflect on the profound impact that a thoughtful, well-balanced diet can have on their health and happiness. This book was crafted with the hope of bringing more than just recipes into your home—it's a manifesto for celebrating the joy and bond shared between you and your canine companion through the food you lovingly prepare.

The journey through the "Healthy Dog Food Cookbook and Food List" was designed to empower you with the knowledge and skills to tailor your dog's diet to their specific needs, ensuring they receive the optimal balance of nutrients to thrive. From the basics of canine nutrition to a diverse collection of recipes that cater to every taste and dietary requirement, our goal has been to provide a comprehensive guide that makes healthy eating accessible and enjoyable for your dog.

By embracing homemade meals, you're choosing to invest in your dog's health, offering them a diet that's free from unnecessary additives and tailored to their unique preferences and nutritional needs. This choice not only has the potential to enhance their physical well-being but also to deepen the bond they share, as each meal becomes an act of love.

Looking forward, the path to maintaining a healthy and joyful life for your dog is an ongoing journey of learning and adaptation. As you continue to explore the world of canine nutrition, remember to observe and listen to your dog's responses to different foods, adjusting as necessary to meet their changing needs. Your relationship with your dog is as unique as the meals you create for them, and this book is just the beginning of a lifelong adventure in health and happiness.

In conclusion, thank you for allowing us to be a part of your journey to discovering the joy of cooking for your dog. May the recipes and meal plans included in this book inspire you to continue exploring the vast world of nutritious, homemade dog food. Here's to the health, vitality, and wagging tails of our furry family members—may they enjoy every bite and every moment spent by your side.

Remember, the most profound gift we can offer our dogs is our time, love, and commitment to their well-being. Let every meal be a reflection of this enduring bond.